# PHARAOHS AND GOVERNMENT

Ancient Egypt History Books Best Sellers

Children's Ancient History

In this book, we're going to talk about the government of Ancient Egypt. So, let's get right to it!

The government of Ancient Egypt was run by the Pharaoh. The Egyptian Pharaoh was not only the leader of the government, he or she was also the religious leader. The Egyptian civilization was very populated so the Pharaoh needed others to help him or her rule and keep order. The government of Ancient Egypt had a hierarchy of rulers, which simply means that some officials were higher ranking than others.

Pharaoh

Pharaoh

# WHAT POWERS DID THE PHARAOH HAVE?

uring the 3,000 years of Ancient Egyptian history, the most powerful and important person was the king. The king, or queen in a few cases, was the Pharaoh who was the top ruler in the land.

Not only was the Pharaoh a political leader, he or she was also the head of the Egyptian religion and was considered the representative of the gods or goddesses on Earth during the performing of religious rituals.

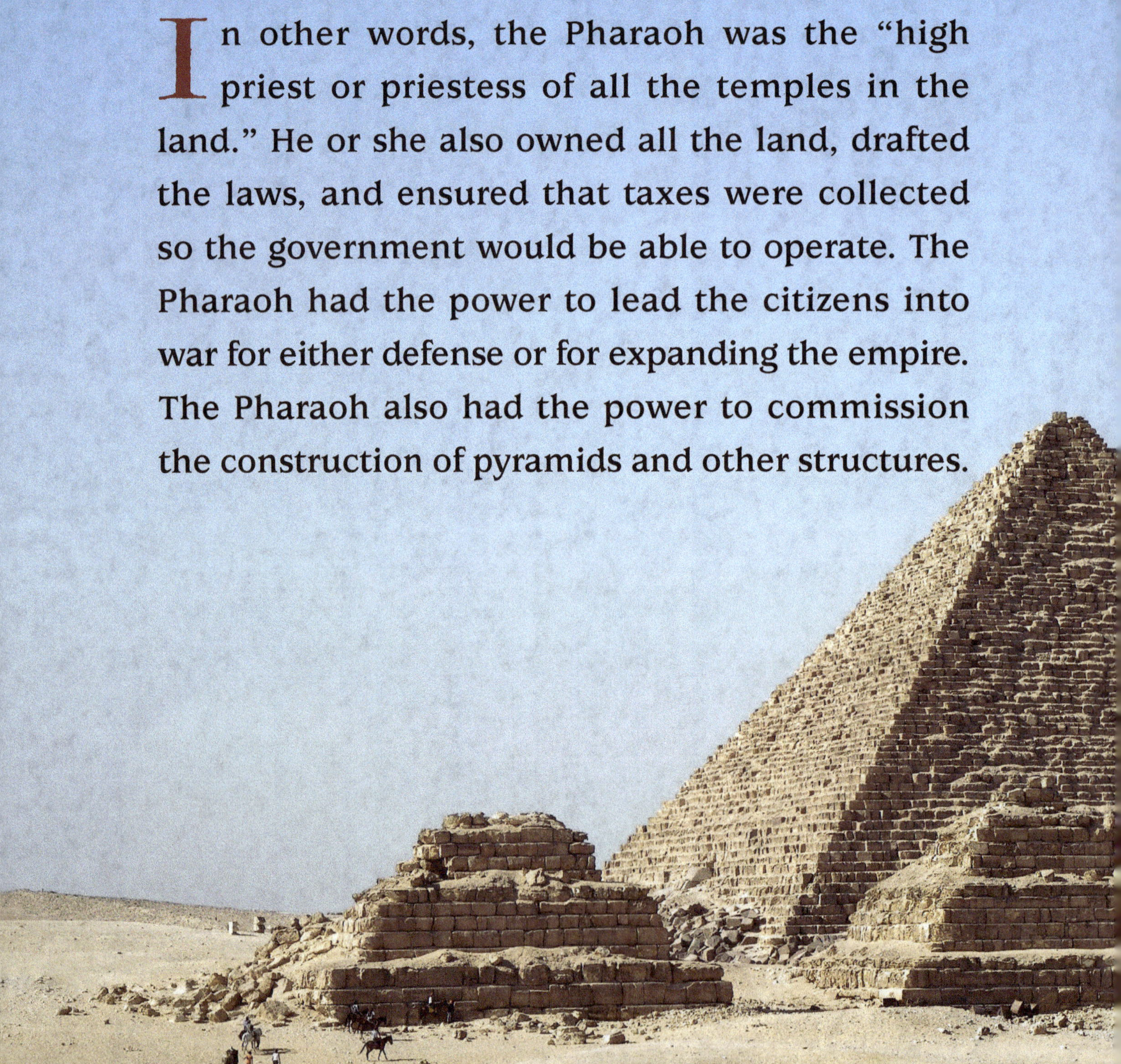

In other words, the Pharaoh was the "high priest or priestess of all the temples in the land." He or she also owned all the land, drafted the laws, and ensured that taxes were collected so the government would be able to operate. The Pharaoh had the power to lead the citizens into war for either defense or for expanding the empire. The Pharaoh also had the power to commission the construction of pyramids and other structures.

Pyramids at Giza

# WHAT WAS THE ROLE OF THE PHARAOH'S WIFE?

Throughout Egypt's history there were three large blocks of time called the Old Kingdom, the Middle Kingdom, and the New Kingdom. During the Old and Middle Kingdoms, the Pharaoh's wife, who was the queen, had many specific duties.

Queen Nefertiti

One of her main functions was to give the Pharaoh as many children as possible, especially sons. The succession of power was much more clear when the Pharaoh had a son or sons to come after him. Others were less apt to try to steal the throne when the family had a line of rulers ready to take the Pharaoh's place. Another function of the queen was to run the palace smoothly and be visible to give support to her husband.

If the Pharaoh died before his son was old enough to rule, she would have acted as regent to run the country until their son came of age. Some women came to full power as Pharaohs in their own right this way, such as Queen Hatshepsut, who eventually took over the position of Pharaoh during the time of the New Kingdom.

Hatshepsut

Statue of Hatshepsut

The trend since the beginning of the New Kingdom was that the queen's role had expanded dramatically. It's more than likely that this happened because there had been a great deal of civil unrest in the previous period. Having a strong queen alongside a strong Pharaoh was one way to give power to the monarchy.

Egypt's Pharaohs had always had more than one wife to ensure that a male heir or heirs were born. During this time, instead of just saying queen, there were different titles. For example, "King's Mother," "King's Great Wife," for his first or favored wife, and "King's Wife" for one of the lesser wives.

Nefertari

Portrait heads of Nefertiti and Akhenaten

Some queens, such as Queen Nefertiti, helped their Pharaoh husbands with policies. She helped her husband Pharaoh Akhenaton propose a new religion.

# WHO WAS THE VIZIER?

The next important leader in the government was the vizier. He acted as the Pharaoh's "right-hand man" and was similar to a prime minister. He was responsible for overseeing all of the Pharaoh's lands, which was basically the entire country of Egypt.

Vizier Kagemni

Imhotep

One of the most famous viziers was Imhotep. He was Pharaoh Djoser's vizier. He was the architect of the very first pyramid and was eventually elevated to the level of a god. Egyptian laws stated that the vizier should always follow the laws, be a fair judge in the courts, control his emotions, and not act in a headstrong manner.

# WHO WERE THE NOMARKS?

Reporting to the vizier were governors who presided over local regions. They were called Nomarks. The province or piece of land they governed was called a nome. The Nomarks were often given their position by the Pharaoh, but sometimes the position was just inherited from generation to generation—father to son.

Scribe

# WHO WERE THE OTHER IMPORTANT GOVERNMENT OFFICIALS?

The commander of the army, the treasurer, and the public works minister were other important officials who had their own responsibilities and powers. No matter what the situation was, the Pharaoh always had the final say on important matters. Scribes and temple priests were an important part of the government.

The priests were crucial to every aspect of daily life in Egypt since religion played an important part in all their actions from birth to death. Scribes were also crucial because they kept the written record of history as well as keeping the financial records. They also helped with the census. The Pharaoh appointed people to act as overseers of the farm land to ensure that the farmers were performing their jobs.

Scribe

# WHAT DID THE GOVERNMENT OF EGYPT DO?

The networks of officials in the government ruled by working together. Every city had officials to ensure that there was order and harmony. The tasks of the government were:

- To keep the countryside peaceful by training and maintaining police

- To hold court for disagreements and to ensure criminals were prosecuted

- To create and maintain a force of soldiers for protection and land acquisition

- To build structures, such as temples for worship and tombs for the afterlife

- To make sure that food was distributed in a fair manner to the people

Pyramid

Nile River

- To collect all appropriate taxes

- To ensure there were records of important events

- To keep the annual records regarding the flooding of the Nile

- To build important businesses like the making of bricks and building of ships

# WHAT HAPPENED WHEN A PHARAOH DIED?

When the Pharaoh passed away, his son would take the throne. If he wasn't old enough to rule, the queen and other high officials in the court would be there to help him rule until he was old enough to rule independently.

Ramses II Tomb

Ancient Egypt

The young heir would have already been well trained in the use of a bow and arrows for hunting. He would need to know how to ride a chariot into battle and how to lead the soldiers in an army. Egypt always had to be ready to defend its land and resources in order to maintain peace and harmony throughout the land.

In its 3,000-year history there were only a few rare cases when a Pharaoh was murdered by one of his own citizens. When it happened, it was because there was a plot at court because the Pharaoh was weak in an area that might have made a difference to Egypt's security. For example, if he was weak in leading the military. Unlike other ancient civilizations, most Pharaohs lived out their lives and calmly ruled the people before dying of old age.

# THE CITIZENS OF EGYPT

Most of the Egyptian population worked in the fields to grow and harvest crops so they could pay their taxes to the Pharaoh. Although they lived in homes, they didn't own their own homes or land.

Those were the property of the Pharaoh. One of the reasons the citizens accepted this situation was because it was a vital part of their religion. The Pharaoh was seen as a god and it was very important never to upset the gods because it could have dire consequences.

In paintings, the Egyptians seem to be happy with their lives. Men and women are working hand and hand in the fields. Their art shows bakers making bread and shipbuilders assembling ships. There seemed to be peace and harmony throughout the land.

Of course, it was part of the Pharaoh's job to maintain this peace by defending Egypt from attacks by foreign lands. Those lands that the Pharaoh conquered would have to bring gifts to their new leader. The gold, storehouses of food, and animals they brought would help fill the Pharaoh's coffers.

Pharaoh

Queen Ty

# FASCINATING FACTS ABOUT THE ANCIENT EGYPTIAN GOVERNMENT

- The Pharaoh's queens, especially his main or favored queen, became more important during the time period of the New Kingdom.

- Taxes were collected every year to help pay for the government and the public works.

- In the New Kingdom, disagreements were settled in court. A group of elders made up a Kenbet, which was something like a modern day jury.

The Pharaoh regularly held court for his top governmental officials. Those who worked for him would approach his throne and kiss the floor in front of his feet.

The Egyptians didn't have complicated laws. In most cases, the judges reviewing a case would rule using common sense and arbitration to get to an agreement.

Awesome! Now you know more about how the Pharaohs ruled Ancient Egypt. You can find more Ancient History books from Baby Professor by searching the website of your favorite book retailer.

Visit
BABY PROFESSOR
EDUCATION KIDS
www.BabyProfessorBooks.com
to download Free Baby Professor eBooks
and view our catalog of new and exciting
Children's Books